Also by JD Viharini

Enjoying India: The Essential Handbook

Travel Fearlessly in India

What Every Woman Should Know

About Personal Safety

JD Viharini

Enjoying India Guides

Second Edition

2020

© 2020-2023 JD Viharini

ISBN: 978-0-9819503-8-9

Foreword

When I first came to India as a tourist in 2000, I was more concerned about getting sick or being scammed than rape or sexual harassment. I researched Indian culture thoroughly before my trip, took precautions, and made sure I dressed in a conservative and smart manner. I was generally treated respectfully and, much to my surprise, even complimented on my attire. However, these days, a growing number of negative media reports about incidents of sexual violence and misconduct in India have created overwhelming safety fears in women's minds.

Personally, I don't feel that India is unsafe for foreign women. It's uncomfortable at times, yes, but not particularly unsafe. Yet, lack of awareness and understanding of Indian culture often unwittingly make foreign women a target of it.

I've lived in India since 2005 and have explored much of the country during the course of my work, writing and managing the content for About.com's India travel website. I'm also married to an Indian man. This has given me some excellent insights into Indian culture. Nevertheless, it's taken me years to unravel it -- and I'm still learning! There are major differences in the way men and women interact in India compared to the west, and the ways I've had to adapt my dress and behavior don't come naturally but are necessary.

Rather than minimizing India's issues and focusing only on the positives, as some writers tend to do, I believe the key is to have realistic expectations and unbiased information. Know what you're likely to encounter and how to deal with it! This will remove fear and give you confidence.

Hence, a practical book about Indian culture is an invaluable resource for foreign women when visiting India. And, I can't think of a better person to write such a book than J D Viharini, a single American woman who's been living in India for more than a decade. She visited India for the first time in 1980 and since then has extensively throughout most of the country by herself, using all modes and classes of transportation, and staying in all types of accommodations (from "Ritz to the pits," as she says). Not only does she know what it's like to travel solo as a foreign woman, she's developed great insight into Indian culture and how the country functions at all levels.

I greatly admire how J D Viharini has integrated herself into Indian society, and the way she shares the vastness and diversity of her experiences. Her life in India has not been insular. She's spent time staying with traditional Indian families and in poor villages. As a result, she's developed a profound and deep understanding of India and Indian culture, which is reflected in her book.

Women's safety is a sensitive topic, and as J D Viharini pertinently points out, "unfortunately quite a few people have the idea that cultural requirements of modesty are a justification for victim-blaming." It's easy to underestimate the importance of dress and respect in Indian culture, especially when Indian women can frequently be seen wearing shorts, skirts, and sleeveless tops in major Indian cities. However, as the book explains in detail, this does not reflect the values of the conservative majority.

Travel Fearlessly in India, What Every Woman Should Know About Personal Safety is a remarkably comprehensive, sensible, and astute book that's packed full of perceptive information, tips and strategies. It covers everything from the mindsets of Indian men and how they conduct themselves to what you need to do if you have to go to the police. It's a book every female should read, and reread, before traveling to India.

— Sharell Cook
India Travel Specialist for About.com and
author of *Henna for the Broken Hearted*

Introduction

The aim of this book is to inspire you and to give you the necessary knowledge and understanding to travel safely in India with confidence, whether you are going solo or traveling with others.

Of course, any time you enter a new culture, you need a good understanding of what's what in order to feel confident and to be able to function well and feel safe. By knowing what to expect and how to prevent problems, you can eliminate constant anxieties and fears about sexual harassment and rape. That is certainly no guarantee that you'll never be afraid. There could be a time when it may be appropriate and even necessary to feel afraid, but it's important to not let your fears control you.

The focus of this book is on preventing problems, which is by far the most important aspect of self-defense. Few of us are martial arts experts who know how to effectively defend ourselves in a physical conflict. However, real self-defense is not so much about defending yourself physically—it's more about knowing how to avoid problems in the first place.

Naturally, many of my tips may be considered common sense—but the 'common' part is questionable. You might say, "Well, that seems obvious," but have you really thought about it before, and have you ever actually done it? If not, then maybe it isn't quite so obvious after all.

You are unlikely to need all my tips and strategies. Getting obsessed with trying to follow all of them is completely unnecessary and would certainly ruin your trip. Figure out what is essential to make you feel comfortable and safe wherever you happen to be at any given time. There are times when you do need to be more careful, so it's important to know what to do.

If you ask Indians about the situation in the area where they live, among people from similar social and economic backgrounds as their own, you usually get reliable information. Beyond that sphere, however, their answers to your questions are likely to be unreliable.

Do ask your Indian friends about safety, but consider their answers in the appropriate context. For instance, if you ask someone from Bangalore about a village in Madhya Pradesh, you are unlikely to get a useful answer because they are extremely different places. There are major differences even within the same city. Asking someone who lives in one of the wealthy enclaves about an area that caters to budget travelers

—or vice versa—is not likely to give you an accurate feel for the situation. They are completely different worlds.

The sole focus of the book is safety. It's not about rights, or what should or shouldn't be. It's about how to deal with conditions in India as they are at present.

India has more cultural diversity than any other country in the world, much of which is different from anything you have experienced elsewhere, so you need a good understanding of what's what in order to be able to function well and feel safe. It's unrealistic to expect to intuitively know everything about how a culture works, but not knowing can lead to unnecessary problems. The advice given here can help you navigate all of India's many cultures.

This book is primarily for women and girls visiting India, as well as those who have decided to stay for a while, whether accompanied or not. Though the practical recommendations are also helpful for Indian women, much of the information is specifically for non-Indians. Sadly, India is generally much less safe for Indian women and girls than for visitors. While on one level, the challenges are much the same, attitudes and social contexts make for significant differences.

India will challenge your every mental and emotional boundary. There's no doubt about that. But it's a good thing because that's what growth is all about. Go ahead and let your boundaries be annihilated. The greatest rewards in life are beyond them.

Don't waste your energy worrying. Never let yourself be ruled by fear. You don't have to be scared of traveling in India. Instead, learn what you need to know; cultivate the right demeanor and attitude; develop good habits; and then get on with enjoying your time in India!

Traveling Fearlessly

You *can* empower yourself to travel fearlessly! There is no reason to let fear stop you from traveling. Sure, traveling always involves some risk, but when it comes to women's safety, the risk of traveling in India may actually be much less than the risk of staying home.

But first of all, you need to understand that fearlessness is not the same as being complacent. It doesn't mean clinging blindly to a "nothing will happen" attitude. Nor does it mean throwing caution to the wind and taking unnecessary risks. What it does mean is freedom from unnecessary worry because you've prepared yourself in advance.

Whenever you feel you have taken sufficient measures to prevent something bad from happening, you stop worrying about it, don't you? Even if you find you can't completely stop worrying, accept that feeling and go ahead anyway. Don't let it control you and dictate how you live your life.

Fearlessness doesn't necessarily mean you never feel fear. Sometimes fear is appropriate. But it's important to understand that there are basically two different kinds of fear. One is that instinctive response to present or imminent danger such as anyone would experience when coming face to face with an angry grizzly bear. Fear brings on the fight-or-flight response that is appropriate when we are faced with a serious immediate threat to our life and wellbeing. This kind of natural fear is necessary to our survival.

Useless fear is anxiety about something that isn't present, of something that hasn't happened, of something that isn't even likely to happen, of something that might not even exist except in our own mind. That's the kind of fear that keeps us from traveling, from doing things we'd like to do, from expanding our boundaries, from going against expectations imposed by others. We don't need such anxieties in our lives because it is far more likely to attract problems than to keep them away. Knowledge is the best weapon against this kind of psychological fear—and the basis for the kind of fearlessness we need to cultivate when we travel. What you put your attention on grows stronger in your life, so keep your attention on what you do want to happen rather than what you don't want.

In this book, you will learn how to avoid becoming a victim of violence. You will also learn how to prevent or minimize non-threatening harassment, as well as how to deal with it if someone does bother you. Traveling fearlessly in India with respect to personal safety is mainly a matter of knowledge and preparation. It's all about confidence that's grounded in knowledge and in reality, not wishful thinking.

Trust Your Intuition

Always relying on others for cues about what to do is foolish. If you always rely on others to keep you safe, you may sometimes find yourself in a situation where you are looking to someone who is totally clueless, who has no concern for your welfare, or who is even planning to harm you. This is why, along with learning the essentials of safety, you need to start trusting your intuition.

Make a habit of noticing the people around you wherever you go. If you see anyone or anything that doesn't feel right, pay more attention and move away. Sometimes there may be nothing that is obviously 'wrong' with a situation or a person, but if your gut feeling is that something doesn't feel right, always go with your feelings and get out. Leave at the first feeling of danger. Don't wait to see what happens. Be as polite and tactful as the situation allows, if for no other reason than to make your exit as easy as possible.

Learning to trust your intuition may take a bit of practice. It's not a skill we are taught, though it really should be. Steve Kardian wrote in his book, *The New Superpower for Women* (which I recommend especially for its excellent information on self-defense):

> *When you are able to trust your gut—that is, actively use your intuition—you are a step ahead.*

Your subconscious mind is wired for safety. It analyzes and processes your surroundings constantly, without your being aware of it, and will send out an alarm when it registers that things are not as they should be. This comes across as a sense of unease and can manifest itself in a variety of locations on the body. We have a whole myriad of expressions, such as "butterflies in your stomach" or a "tingling" on your skin, that reflect the different ways your brain communicates with you through physical sensations. By training yourself to pay attention, you can notice the messages your subconscious is broadcasting. The good news is that through practice, you can strengthen and develop your intuition. It is the most basic form of self-defense and one of the most powerful tools you have to stay out of harm's way.[1]

---

[1] Kardian, Steve. *The New Superpower for Women: Trust Your Intuition, Predict Dangerous Situations, and Defend Yourself from the Unthinkable* (p. 2). Touchstone. Kindle Edition.

Is India Dangerous?

Given recent news from India, you might have the impression that India is an incredibly dangerous place for women to travel. That is just not true. Although, as with anywhere else, women have to exercise a certain amount of care and vigilance, violent crime against foreign tourists is relatively rare. If you come to India knowing the essentials of staying safe—and if you are sensible, alert, and respectful of the culture—there is really little risk of being the victim of sexual violence.

Fear of rape is simply not a reason to avoid India. In fact, you may be much safer from sexual assault here than in your own country.[2]

Attacks on foreign tourists always make the headlines in a big way, but don't be put off by the bad press. There are generally no more than two or three dozen such reports a year, which puts the number of reported rapes of foreign tourists in India at hardly 1

---

[2] "India's 'Rape Epidemic': An Ugly Colonial Myth Reborn," Sadhvi Sharma, http://www.spiked-online.com/newsite/article/indias-rape-epidemic-an-ugly-colonial-myth-reborn/16781

in 100,000[3], given the number of people who visit the country annually. Compare that with the US, for instance, where more than 24 rapes per 100,000 are reported. While it's obvious that many rapes are not reported to the police in either country, this still gives a reasonable idea of the relative risk. Also, most rapes are not committed by strangers, which is the reality in most countries, not only in India.

Because the media likes to portray India as a particularly dangerous place for women to visit, it's necessary to put the risk factor in perspective. This is not to deny that there is a problem—though it's a global one, not just an Indian one—or to trivialize it in any way. Although progress is painfully slow, the growing outrage of Indians is starting to bring about a much-needed change of attitude, and more positive action on the part of the government.

Men should behave decently, and most usually do; but since some don't, we have to be proactive about our own security. While violent assaults against non-

---

'Crime in India', an annual release of the home ministry's National Crime Records Bureau (NCRB), has for the first time collected, collated and published statistics of crimes committed against foreigners and by foreigners in India. While the category known as 'foreign tourists' has been specified, foreigners living in the country on business visas, or as students, or as long-stay visitors have been clubbed under the category 'other than tourist foreigners'.

In 2015, there were around 8,000,000 tourist arrivals. Foreigners have been accused in 12 cases of rape, while 19 have been victims.

Indian women are relatively rare in India, other forms of sexual harassment are not uncommon. In any case, if you are careful and sensible and project a confident, fearless attitude, you are really unlikely to run into serious problems.

What precautions you need to take depends on many factors: whether you are alone or with someone (and who you are with), the location, how and when you are traveling, and any festivals or special events that may be going on at the time.

It's possible for even single women to travel around India alone without being constantly harassed. Nevertheless, while some places are really safe, others may require you to take considerably more precautions. There are a few places where there is ongoing unrest that should be avoided altogether, but most everywhere else in the country is generally quite manageable with the appropriate amount of caution. Find out about places before you go, and when you arrive, talk to the locals to get a feel for the situation there.

The first time I came to India alone, I was a little nervous. I had been to India before, so I already knew quite a lot about the culture and what I needed to do to stay safe, but I had been hearing that it wasn't safe to travel alone in India. To my surprise, I quickly found that I felt much safer in India than in the US— and that's still the case. Altogether, I've spent more than 15 years in India, mostly on my own, but I have never experienced anything more than occasional mild harassment, and never any actual threat.

About Indian Men

Even though sexual harassment is not uncommon, especially in tourist areas, it's actually only a small percentage of men who go around harassing women. Most Indian men will help you and treat you with respect, especially if you present yourself as someone deserving it. But, unfortunately, you can't just forget about the others.

Since in India there are relatively few opportunities for sex outside of marriage, many men feel extreme sexual pressure and frustration, so it's foolish to unnecessarily inflame those feelings. Because the society is so conservative, Indian men can get aroused by modes of dress and behaviors that would be considered normal in most other countries. The trouble is that if a man gets aroused by the way you dress or act, it's not just his problem. It becomes your problem if he thinks you're inviting sex when you aren't. This is not to excuse inappropriate action, but rather an understanding of the expectations of the local culture.

It is common for Indian men to work far from their homes, and many only see their wives once a month or even once a year, which adds significantly to their frustration. This is not only the case for unskilled and domestic workers, but also for many who travel for business or who work in the tourism sector.

Instead of taking responsibility for their own behavior, men who are lacking in self-control often put forth the specious, self-serving excuse that women are weak because they can't resist trying to seduce men! An absurd argument, indeed, yet it is accepted by much of Indian society. But however unfair it is that men blame women for their own weaknesses, we can't ignore the fact that they are prone to getting easily aroused, and they don't always control their urges.

The cultural norm in most of India is for women to keep a safe distance from men, especially strangers. Most Indian men wouldn't approach Indian girls as casually as they might approach non-Indians, because doing so would be seen as an insult. They may think it doesn't matter because, as foreigners, we are presumed to be unaware of the insult.

Unfortunately, it's always necessary to be on your guard with men you don't know or are just getting to know, no matter how nice they seem. Sometimes the most charming ones are the worst con artists. You are more likely to meet up with men of this sort in the major tourist areas. There are always some who are out to get whatever they can.

Traditionally, Indian men are taught not to touch women even accidentally. A hand brushing your breast or hip is usually deliberate. Of course, there's no safe distance on a crowded bus or train, but even so, men should manage to keep their hands away from a woman's most sensitive parts. I'll go into what you can do to protect yourself in a later chapter.

It's usually better not to tell men you don't know well exactly where you are staying, unless you definitely want them coming around.

Avoid interacting with groups of men, even to ask directions. Men who hang out in packs are often insecure and they may feel they have to prove something to their buddies.

But don't worry. This is not to say that you should never talk to Indian men. Not at all. Just be alert and use good sense. And never ignore any gut feeling you might have that something is off.

Be Careful With Fellow Travelers, Too

Be cautious with new friends you make on your travels, whether Indian or not. Most of us tend to gravitate toward others from our own or similar cultures as a refuge in an unfamiliar world, but that's not a reason to automatically trust them. Enjoy their company, but do be alert, especially if something feels a little off. Try not to be too hasty about letting your guard down with someone you have just met, whether he's Indian or from your own country.

Even if you've been hanging out with someone for a while, remember that you are seeing him out of context. As far as you are concerned, he has no history except for what he has told you, which could easily be a fabrication. Don't worry about it, but do pay attention.

It's best not to reveal too many details about yourself and your travel plans when you are just getting to know someone. Get him to talk about himself rather than talking too much about about yourself—and really listen to what he says.

How Indians See Us

The Indian media tends to portray foreign women as promiscuous, so this is the predominant impression a lot of Indians have. For many Indian men, especially those from rural areas or who are not well educated, what they see on the screen is all they know about us. As a result, some men think it's OK to treat foreign women like prostitutes, especially when their dress and demeanor are indecent by local standards. The fact that some women do come to India looking for sex contributes to the impression that we are all like that.

It doesn't help that most Bollywood movies portray women as sex objects. Storylines often have the hero teasing and harassing his leading lady until she blissfully accepts him as the love of her life. It gives some men the idea that this is the way girls secretly want to be treated—and that this is the way women should be treated.

When women from less conservative countries dress and act as if they were back home, they often don't realize that they are doing anything inappropriate, especially when they see others doing the same.

Even in cosmopolitan settings where it appears that "everyone" is dressing or acting in ways that don't reflect the values of the much more conservative majority, there are always people in the background who are likely to get turned on or offended by behaviors and manners of dress that wouldn't be considered provocative back home.

This cultural context makes a huge difference and you can't ignore it, even if your cosmopolitan friends and associates like to believe that they themselves are completely disassociated from traditional Indian life. Many affluent Indians simply do not consider those they regard as being lower in status—which means the vast majority—in their thinking. They go about their lives without really seeing them.

Do be aware that men from the upper economic classes often have a tendency to feel entitled to take whatever they want. In other words, it's good to be mindful of all the men around you. Sexual abusers can belong to any class.

One thing you must accept is that you will inevitably get stared at, by women as well as men. Staring isn't necessarily harassment. It's often just that Indians are curious about us and want to understand how our lives are different from theirs. But staring back at men could be misinterpreted as an invitation, so just look away.

Fair skin is highly prized in India, and Indian men are often strongly attracted to women with light complexions. If you are fair, especially if you are also young and blond, you will often find people taking your photo, either openly or secretly. You may start to feel like a celebrity with all the attention.

In some ways, a light complexion can be an advantage. Even though we don't really fit into the Indian social structure, Westerners in general and Caucasians in particular are believed to be rich and therefore, by inference, powerful, which gives us a certain status. The risk of rape may be much less because of that status, as it can give the idea that the consequences might be particularly severe.

Sadly, the British occupation left Indians with an unrealistic preference for light skin. One particularly unfortunate consequence of this is that a dark complexion can attract more harassment in many parts of India, especially in the north.

Essentials of Prevention

Mental preparation is the most important aspect of prevention. Cultivate the right attitude and demeanor; make a habit of being alert and in the present; understand and respect the culture; and always know where you are.

Act confident even if you don't feel it. It's essential to project an image of someone who deserves respect and can take care of herself. An appearance of confidence and purposefulness is enough to deflect much potential harassment. Stand tall and hold your head high.

Be confidently cool and aloof with men you don't know. Smile at the world, but don't direct friendly looks to strange men. Avoid looking men in the eye, even in passing, as this can be seen as an indication that you are out looking for sex. (Seriously!) When you pass men on the street, especially groups, give a brief, uninterested, even dismissive, glance, and then immediately look away with an air of indifference.

It's OK to ignore random questions from passing strangers. You may like to respond to questions from women and children, but it's best to ignore ones from men.

Be alert to what's going on around you, especially when you are out and about. Don't move around while texting, listening to music or talking on the phone, especially with a headset on. Keep your awareness in the present. Whenever you need to text or talk on your cell phone, find a safe place to sit down and do it—a place where no one can sneak up on you without your knowing. Always be aware of your surroundings. You'll enjoy your time in India more, too—and there's so much to enjoy.

Print out or write down contact details and directions wherever you are headed. Unfortunately, you can't always depend on having constant Internet access, especially away from the metro areas.

Always know where you are. Get local maps or download them on your smartphone—and use them. But try to avoid standing around on the street trying to figure out where you are. It's better to go into a store or cafe. Moving around without paying attention to your surroundings makes you an easy target—not to mention that it puts you at risk from careless drivers, which is actually a much greater danger.

If you stop to take a selfie, look around before you do and don't let it take your awareness away from your surroundings. Getting absorbed in the process makes you exceptionally vulnerable. Incidentally, thieves love selfie sticks because it's so easy to snatch them, especially from people who are too absorbed in taking selfies to notice anything going on around them.

Avoid accepting food or drink from strangers, especially on trains or buses or around major tourist sites. Although it's not so common, instances of travelers being drugged and robbed are not unknown. When people offer, it is best to thank them, while politely and firmly declining. A smile and simple hand gesture are usually sufficient. Most people understand and are not offended. However, if someone has ill intentions, he or she may pretend to feel hurt by your refusal and your lack of trust. This may be an act. You're not declining their hospitality in their own home, and you certainly have no obligation to trust someone you've just met. Even if you have been sitting together for several hours and they offer something that appears unopened, or if they take a cookie from a package before offering some to you, it's usually best to politely decline.

Indians are fabulously hospitable people, but you may sometimes find yourself in situations where you really don't want to eat or drink anything for one reason or another. The surest way to decline hospitality without offending anyone is to say, "I'm fasting just now." Maybe you will break your fast as soon as you are out of their sight, but they don't need to know that. Fasting is understood all over India as it is common for people to fast both for religious and health reasons. Most people won't even ask why you are fasting.

Incidentally, taking tea in a reputable shop is generally quite safe, especially if there are other customers. If you have any doubts, politely decline.

Ignore beggars and touts; they will keep following you and harassing you if you show even the slightest interest in them. Also, if you give anything to one beggar, you are likely to be surrounded by many more and that can get scary. Never go anywhere with a tout.

Be evasive and avoid answering overly personal questions. If you are alone, avoid saying so. Many solo travelers like to wear a wedding band, and some carry a photo of their 'husband' as well. It can certainly be a useful ploy, and many people swear by it, but truthful evasions are less complicated. If you decide to pretend you are married, think out your story in advance so you don't embarrass yourself. You will inevitably be bombarded with questions like, "Where is he? What does he do? Why isn't he with you? When is he coming? What about your children?" and so on.

Personally, I often just say that I'm never alone and leave it at that. I don't bother to explain what I mean. Sometimes I just vaguely say that my friends or family are 'around', without specifying where. As I feel that the whole world is my family, it's entirely true from my perspective, though it's not quite what they are thinking. Another evasive strategy that I use a lot is to turn the tables and ask the questioner about himself. It's a good distraction because most people love to talk about themselves.

Find out as much as you can about a place before you go there. Check on the local news occasionally to find out if there is some big demonstration or festival planned, or anything else you might need to know about.

Don't walk alone at night, and avoid walking alone in isolated or bad areas even in the daytime. If you aren't comfortable with the area, carry some pepper spray. You can buy it in all major cities in India. You'll probably never need it, but having it at hand does add a feeling of security. You are more likely to need pepper spray for aggressive monkeys and mad dogs than men, but it can be a lifesaver if you find yourself in a sticky situation somewhere.

Although I carry it most of the time, I've only ever used my pepper spray on a monkey, apart from one time I had to hold it in a man's face to get him to go away. He wasn't actually out to assault me; but he did grab my arm in an aggressive way to try to make me give him more money than we had agreed on for the taxi fare. He didn't know what I was threatening him with, but he realized it was probably something quite unpleasant, and after looking at it for a couple of minutes, he stalked off. If he had asked politely, we might have given him something, but grabbing a woman like that was way out of line.

It's best not to wear expensive clothes, jewelry or other accessories, except for specific occasions where it's appropriate. Even then, you may want to tone it down a little. Looking wealthy can attract too much of the wrong kind of attention.

Keep your passport, money, credit cards, etc. in an inner pocket or money pouch, but be sure you can access them easily and modestly. Or, if you keep your wallet in a daypack, use the inmost pocket and an attachment of some kind, such as a wallet with a theft-proof cable that you can attach to the inside of the bag. Try to avoid keeping your daypack on your back if you are in a crowd. Sling it over one shoulder and put your arm over it or carry it in front.

Always carry enough cash to get back to where you are staying, and then some. Don't keep all your money in one place.

Avoid using ATMs at night. The safest ATMs are the ones inside banks or that have guards posted. And of course you should always be aware of who else is around when you are using the ATM, and whether they seem to be too interested in you.

Always carry a flashlight at night. Power outages are frequent all over India, and you don't want to be caught outside without a light. A small keychain flashlight is convenient, because you can keep it with you all the time; so if you are unexpectedly out late, you at least have that much light.

You may have lots of strangers asking to take a photo with you. It's really common and usually quite innocuous. If it's a group of boys, they may just be looking for an excuse to put their arms around you; and you could even end up getting groped or pinched. It's OK to say 'no'.

A useful strategy if you are really tired of overly enthusiastic photographers is to tell them you charge a modeling fee, collected in advance. Many locals ask for money from tourists who take their photo, so there's no reason you can't turn the tables. Few people would even consider taking you up on it; but even if they do, it doesn't give them the right to put their hands on you.

By far, the biggest risk to personal safety in India is actually the traffic rather than people, so pay attention to it whenever you are on the street. Walking or driving while talking on the phone, texting, taking selfies or listening to music is even more dangerous in India than most places. As Indians drive on the left, it's usually best to walk or jog on the right side of the road, facing the traffic, but do be aware of traffic coming up behind you. Indians don't always bother about being on the right side of the street.

You also have to be careful of monkeys and street dogs. Packs of street dogs can be dangerous, particularly at night, so avoid them. Monkeys may try to steal anything you are carrying, or even the glasses off your face, but they may also bite. If you get bitten or scratched by either a dog or a monkey (or any other animal, for that matter), go immediately to the nearest hospital. Incidentally, if a monkey steals something, they will almost always drop it if you throw some food for them—monkeys around tourist areas generally have an excellent understanding of ransom!

Never let anyone ridicule or manipulate you into abandoning your good security habits. Trust your own feelings about what you need to do to feel safe.

Safe Interactions with Indian Men

If a man seems to be misinterpreting your intentions, let him know it immediately. Get away from men who ignore your personal space and try to cozy up to you when you haven't invited it.

Learn to be reserved with strange men, while at the same time radiating a confident feeling of universal friendliness. This attitude is a much better protection than being wary and tense, which can attract the wrong kind of attention because it makes you look weak and vulnerable. This may take a bit of cultivation, but the rewards are worth it. It is said that the world is as you are, so this means that radiating friendliness to everyone around you will generally make the people you meet and your environment friendlier toward you.

Flirting and wearing sexy clothes is not a normal part of Indian culture, and of the way men and women relate to each other. Dressing or acting in a way that is designed to be sexually attractive unintentionally invites trouble. If you dress or act in a sexually provocative manner, don't be surprised if men try to grope you, etc. You'll be regarded as fair game. Of course, we should be able to dress in ways that make us feel good about ourselves without men getting the wrong idea, but this is about the situation as it exists today, not about the ideal that doesn't.

Avoid flirting with a man unless you want to end up in bed with him. Flirting is not taken as innocent fun in India. It's usually seen as a definite invitation for sex. Even casual conversations with men you meet in passing, such as on a train, may be misinterpreted and lead to unwanted sexual advances. Be reserved in such situations and avoid answering personal questions about yourself. If the conversation turns to sex, shut him out and leave.

Men who are intent on rape try to isolate their victims. Avoid accepting unsolicited help from men who come up and offer to show you around, help you find something, etc. Just ignore them and keep moving. If you do accept anyone's offer to show you the way somewhere, be alert. Don't follow blindly or go where there's no one around or where there are only men. And don't go with a group of men.

If you need to ask for directions, be discriminating about who you approach for information. Avoid approaching groups of men, beggars, touts, or rough-looking people. It's much better to go into a decent shop or restaurant if there is no one on the street you feel comfortable talking to.

Try to avoid situations where you will be alone with Indian men. Your willingness to be alone with a man even in innocent situations may be misinterpreted as an invitation for greater intimacy. Do not allow men to come into your room, or go into theirs, unless that's what you want. If you need a repairman to come, try to have someone else there with you, or at least leave the door open while he is there.

While a head massage by a man in a busy salon is OK, a full-body massage in a private room definitely isn't. Always insist on having a woman do the massage.

Even in offices and other professional situations, be careful about being alone with a man. Unfortunately, it's necessary to be alert for indications that men are getting unwelcome ideas even in situations where you wouldn't expect it.

Avoid the guys who go after beautiful young girls by posing as talent scouts for Bollywood or modeling agencies. Even if they provide some sort of 'proof' of their identity (which can be easily faked), just don't go there. But if you are convinced they are legitimate and do want to check their offer out, don't go alone or only with another girl who might be a target. Keep a friend with you the whole time.

Don't hesitate to approach and make friends with local women. A big smile is often enough to break the ice. Ask them about local customs and the safest ways of doing things. If you are being harassed, do reach out to any women who may be around.

Whenever you go out at night, tell someone where you are going and when you expect to be back. Avoid staying out late unless you are with someone you know and trust.

It's not uncommon for predators the world over to use social media sites to find their victims, so be wary of friend requests from men you don't know. Should you decide you want to meet up with someone you met on social media, don't go alone, and do meet in a public place. Remember, con artists are almost always charming people who seem really nice—that's why they are so successful at fooling people.

Connecting for Safety

Keep people informed of your whereabouts. If you have a pre-planned itinerary, send it to friends or family members and try to include telephone numbers where you can be reached. Be in touch with someone regularly. If you are planning something risky, let someone know the details.

Smartphones are a great asset when it comes to personal safety[4]. If you have one, take the time to program all your important contact numbers into it, including the national emergency numbers:

Fire, Police, Ambulance :	112
Women's helpline:	181
Tourist helpline,:	1363
Childline:	1098

Be sure to keep a backup of all your contacts on paper and online, as well, in case you lose your phone.

There are a number of safety apps for women in India that you might consider putting on your phone. Check your app store for the current offerings.

Get in the habit of sending photos of people you are hanging out or traveling with, along with their names and other information. Do it in the spirit of fun for the

---

[4] Of course, there are health issues, so there's definitely a tradeoff.

purpose of preserving your memories, but be aware that this habit could be a lifesaver if you run into problems. Using a smartphone with an Indian SIM and a data plan (which is extremely cheap), you can send photos as soon as you take them.

In case you are alone and feeling unsafe—if, for instance, someone is following you or watching you with too much interest—don't be afraid to ask other women or families if you can tag along with them. Indians will almost always welcome you, and you may end up making new friends while you are at it. If language barriers prevent an explanation, just stay near them anyway.

The Need for Respect

Many women unknowingly make themselves a target of unnecessary harassment simply because they don't understand the culture. Learning how to avoid major cultural blunders will go a long way toward keeping you safe.

Fortunately, most Indians don't expect visitors to be perfectly tuned in to the nuances of the local culture, but if you do your best to be respectful, people will notice, and in turn you will be treated with greater respect. Respecting the standards of the local culture can greatly reduce the risk of sexual harassment.

If you dress and behave in a way that is sufficiently modest to honor the local standards, you won't stand out in a bad way. Do your best to get into the habit of dressing, speaking and behaving more modestly than you would at home.

Smoking, drinking, using drugs and swearing are habits that are generally regarded as being indications of a loose moral character in women almost everywhere in the country. Be aware that doing these things in public reinforces the negative stereotype people have of foreign women. Strong profanity is regarded as disrespectful, so if you are in the habit of swearing a lot, do your best to tone down your language.

If you behave intimately with your partner in public (hugging, kissing, or fondling each other), you may be unwittingly sending a message to passers-by that you are a sex-starved woman who may be available to anyone, even if you have no eyes for anyone else. Even holding hands is too much in many places. Save your intimacies—as well as your sexy clothes and flirtatious behavior—for when you are alone together.

It's easy to get confused about what's appropriate in any given place because rather than a single, homogeneous culture that pervades the whole country, there are more than a hundred distinct cultures, many of which have little in common with each other.

Nevertheless, India's many cultures and subcultures are generally quite conservative, which means that women are expected to dress and act modestly just about everywhere. Unfortunately, many people have the idea that cultural requirements of modesty are a justification for victim-blaming; but that is a narrow, over-simplified view that doesn't take other important factors into account.

Many cultures have conservative standards of dress and behavior that have evolved over countless generations, and the reasons behind them are complex. To assume, for instance, that traditional women's clothing is solely about blaming women for men's sexual misconduct is a mistake. While that might be an underlying aspect in many cases, it's essential to understand that traditional dress is an essential aspect of cultural identity, which is an extremely complex matter. It's not for us to judge when we don't know the whole story. In any case, cultural identity should be respected and preserved. It would be tragic for India to lose its cultural diversity, which is one of the things that make it so wonderful.

Westerners are often critical of certain aspects of Indian society, not all of which are deserving of criticism. Some people assume, for instance, that all Indian women are oppressed and long to behave and dress as Westerners do. While that may apply to some women, it certainly doesn't apply to all. India is not an individualistic society, and there is no reason why it must become one. Western standards are suitable for the West, not for India. It creates more problems when outsiders who don't understand a society and the value of its customs attempt to impose change because they think only their values are valid. Respecting the culture as you find it is an essential aspect of staying safe, as Indians can be extraordinarily touchy about their cultural values.

As Alvaro Enterria so aptly put it in his book, *India From Within*: "Consciously or unconsciously, the idea that Western values are the universally valid human values prevails in the West. But to attempt to use our parameters and ways of thinking to judge or attempt to understand a society and culture that, being based on very different principles, eludes our grasp, is to run the serious risk of not understanding anything."[5]

In order to even begin to understand Indian society, it's necessary to understand the concept of *izzat*, which is fundamental to social interactions in India. *Izzat* is one's honor, as well as one's self-respect, one's self-esteem. Moreover, there is also a collective *izzat* that belongs to families, clans, castes, the various Indian cultures, tribes, religious groups, political parties, and, of course, the nation as a whole. How much respect is given to a person or group is determined by strict but unwritten hierarchical rules, which every Indian learns from infancy. These rules govern all aspects of behavior in India, and how individuals and groups relate to each other.

If one fails to give the respect that a person feels is due to himself, his religion, his family, etc., it "...can provoke an irrational response totally disproportionate to the level of the slight."[6] Fortunately, most Indians are pretty tolerant and forgiving of ignorant mistakes on the part of visitors.

---

5 Alvaro Enterria, *India From Within*, Indica Books, Varanasi, 2010, p.18

6 Pavan K. Varma, *Being Indian*, Penguin Books, New Delhi, 2004, pp. 39–40.

However, when visitors go around flagrantly disrespecting cultural norms, either out of ignorance or prejudice, or because they simply don't care, or even because they have the misguided idea that they are somehow helping to 'liberate' Indian women, they are insulting the collective honor. Whether they realize it or not, they are also undermining their own honor and showing themselves to be undeserving of respect. They offend many people and attract unnecessary harassment. This kind of behavior also reflects poorly on the collective honor of the visitors' own country.

One thing that can up the respect factor is to get your clothes neatly pressed. In most places there are *press-walas* who will iron your clothes for a few rupees, and it's worth taking advantage of their services whenever you can. A person who is well-dressed is more highly regarded than someone whose appearance is sloppy or dirty. If you go around looking grubby, you won't get much respect. Avoid clothes that the locals think of as being appropriate for lower classes even if you think they look cool. And please avoid walking around on the streets barefoot. (This is also important for health reasons as you can pick up some really nasty parasites from going barefoot on the streets and other unclean places.) Do your best to be as neat and clean as you can at all times. If you don't have time to wash your clothes, you are moving too fast.

It's impossible to overstate the value of respect in how you are treated in India—and it goes both ways. As well as showing that you are deserving of respect, dressing well is seen in the Indian culture as something that shows respect. Look around and you will see that almost all women make the effort to look as good as they can in their circumstances. Diane Sharma Winter expresses it well:

> *Indians totally appreciate a well turned out woman and usually treat you differently once you have passed their initial assessment. In most situations Indians assess the character of a person by the cut of their cloth, instantly and instinctively. This is not so much snobbish as it is cultural in origin. Traditionally in India, caste and position were immediately obvious by the way in which a person dressed. From the placement of jewelry to the length of a turban, the dress code in India is so intricately wedded into the DNA of the average Indian that it's impossible to decode....* [7]

Indians won't usually tell you if you are doing something they consider inappropriate—but they will definitely notice. If it's something that has caused them to lose respect for you, they will probably try to hide their lack of respect out of natural politeness or

_____

[7] Diane Sharma Winter http://www.womentravelmotherindia.com/what-to-wear-in-india-the-rule-of-the-three-bs/

cultural conditioning. Nevertheless, it will still affect how you are received. People tend to respond to you as you present yourself.

The Basic Indian Dress Code

How you dress profoundly affects how people respond to you, and this is perhaps even more so in India than in most other countries.

Although we shouldn't have to worry about men getting the wrong idea because of our clothes, the practical reality is that honoring local standards of dress definitely helps. Unfortunately, as foreigners, we are already at a disadvantage due to common misconceptions, so it is important to dress conservatively.

Girls who dress and act modestly are more highly regarded than those who flout the cultural norms, and they are safer from sexual harassment. If you dress immodestly according to local standards, some people will inevitably treat you like a slut. Dressing modestly won't guarantee that you will never be harassed, but you'll almost certainly get harassed less.

Since standards vary from place to place, you can look around at how most of the local women dress (not the tourists), and cover up to a similar extent. Nevertheless, in spite of the differences from place to place, there is a kind of basic Indian dress code that is acceptable virtually everywhere. It's important to understand the fundamental concept, along with the reasons behind it, because it's an essential part of projecting an image of someone who deserves respect. If you don't want to always have to think about what to wear, you can just follow the general guidelines below to feel comfortable anywhere in India.

Basic standards of modesty almost everywhere in India require that you cover your knees, upper arms, shoulders, cleavage and midriff, though the standards are even more conservative in many areas. Tops should not show your cleavage or be too tight or revealing. Leave your sheer blouses, shorts, spaghetti-strap dresses, bikinis, tank tops, etc. at home. Wearing clothing that is indecent by local standards is insulting to the culture. It also gives men the idea that you are "available"—even if your behavior clearly indicates the opposite.

Ultimately, what kind of clothes you choose to wear is not as important as how you wear them. While it's acceptable to wear Western clothes almost everywhere, it's essential to wear them in a manner that is respectful to the very modest Indian culture. However, there are some exceptionally conservative places where you may be better off wearing traditional Indian clothes. Also, there are a few temples where ladies will not be admitted unless they are wearing a *sari* (not to mention a few where foreigners aren't allowed at all), though Western clothes are acceptable in most temples as long as they are modest.

Some people argue that since Indians are used to seeing Westerners dressed however they like, and since Western dress is the so-called 'international standard' of dress, it's ridiculous to worry about what you wear. Others feel that maintaining their personal style is more important than whether anyone is offended by it, no matter what the context. And there are those who think that no one has a right to feel offended because they don't feel offended by what anyone else wears. I disagree.

The notion that there is an international standard of dress that should be considered universally acceptable is unrealistic—and it's disrespectful of many cultures throughout the world. In India, family and society are generally considered much more important than individuality, so it's best to refrain from asserting your individuality in a way that is offensive to the local culture.

While researching this book, I spoke with many women about their experiences with Indian men. Those who did not respect the Indian standards of dress almost invariably reported more problems with harassment.

For the vast majority of Indians, the basic standards of modesty are compulsory. It's true that many girls and women—especially in major tourist places and big cities like Mumbai, Delhi, and Goa—tend to dress in ways that are considered immodest by traditional standards, but they are not in the majority in most of the country. For now, this is the reality.

Indian men generally prefer to see modestly dressed women, both because such attire shows respect for the culture, and because it doesn't put unnecessary strain on their self-control. Most Indians, including women, are embarrassed to see women wearing skimpy clothes. To my surprise, on two or three occasions men have come up to me on the street and thanked me for dressing modestly and respecting their culture! This was, as you might expect, in a conservative area where many female tourists dress inappropriately by local standards—and some even by most Western standards.

If you are in a cosmopolitan environment where you have little direct contact with more traditional Indians, you may feel that you can safely wear whatever you please, but I would still advise you to dress fairly conservatively for reasons mentioned above.

In order to make yourself less of a target, it is advisable to avoid looking like a tourist, even if you are one. This is something that experts recommend for travel everywhere, and it is certainly important in India. It's not about trying to disguise the fact that you are a foreigner. Most of us couldn't do so, anyway. But save the souvenir clothes such as the Taj Mahal T-shirts for when you get home.

In spite of their great popularity, it's also better to avoid the cheap, hippyish clothes made for tourists that Indians seldom wear. They mark you as a tourist just as clearly as the souvenir T-shirts do.

Form-fitting yoga wear is not appropriate for wear in public. Save it for the yoga studio or your room, or wear something more modest over it.

Though sleeveless tops are fairly common in some places during the hot season, in most others they are not considered acceptable. It's better to at least cover your upper arms. Surprisingly, while you might think it would make you feel too hot, being fully covered with loose, lightweight cotton or linen clothes can actually be cooler and more comfortable than going around with bare arms and legs. The Indian sun can be brutal.

It's acceptable for your midriff to be exposed when wearing a sari, but not otherwise. Shorts and short skirts are generally not acceptable. A bra is essential, but underwear should not show at all.

When wearing pants, loose, tunic-style tops that cover your buttocks and crotch are ideal. A long, not-too-tight T-shirt also works. Though many of us like to wear our tops neatly tucked in, it's better to let them hang out. It's also cooler in the hot weather.

Your swimsuit should be conservative, no matter where you plan to wear it. Although there are certain beaches, especially in Goa, where you might get the impression that everyone wears bikinis, if you look around for a while, you'll see that it's not really so. In any case, on the way to or from the beach or pool, or whenever you are interacting with locals, put on something modest over your swimsuit. Incidentally, swimming or sunbathing alone on a remote beach is not a good idea, no matter what you are wearing.

Aside from small children and *naga babas*[8], public nudity is unacceptable everywhere, so a swimsuit or other clothes must be worn even when bathing in a remote location. Underwear is absolutely not acceptable bathing attire for women, though men can get away with it. Oh, that double standard again!

If you have long hair, consider wearing it tied back or up in some way. Leaving it loose can be seen as immodest.

Girls who wear traditional Indian clothes often report that they receive more respect than when they wear Western dress. It also serves as a great icebreaker. Many people will comment on it, and you will find that the comments are almost always positive because it shows your appreciation of their culture.

Incidentally, well-cut Indian suits and well-draped *saris* flatter just about every figure—much better than most Western clothes—not to mention the fact that

---

[8] Naked *sadhus* or holy men.

they are incredibly comfortable when made of natural fabrics. Really lightweight cottons are especially well-suited to the climate.

There are several varieties of ladies' pantsuits. For traditional salwar and *churidhar* suits, a scarf (*chunni* or *dupatta*) draped across the front is an essential part of the outfit, so don't leave it off.

For a more international look, get the pants made with a straight leg; or else buy ready-made tops to wear over your Western-style pants. A long *kurta* over wide-legged palazzo pants or a *lehenga* (long, full skirt) is another popular style, one that can be either dressy or casual. These looks are more flexible in terms of the scarf. You can wear it however you like or even dispense with it altogether without making the outfit look all wrong. However, it's good to carry a scarf or shawl no matter what you are wearing in case you need it to protect your face from dust, or if you wish to go into a temple, etc. And in conservative places, it's good to wear it anyway to honor the local standards of modesty.

Hassle-Free Arrival

Always book your first night in advance even if you plan to be completely spontaneous the rest of the time. Airport Metro and bus connections don't run late at night, so if you arrive at night, definitely arrange for someone to pick you up at the airport, especially if you are traveling alone. It's wonderfully comforting to have someone standing at the airport exit with your name on a placard when you arrive. Be sure to get the name and mobile number of the driver meeting you so you can call him if necessary. At the airport, you can buy an Indian SIM card or make a call from a public phone booth. Confirm your reservation and your pickup in advance.

At airports, bus and railway stations, and tourist sites, many taxi and auto-rickshaw drivers, touts, and even porters solicit travelers with offers of ridiculously cheap transportation, tours, houseboats and hotels. Avoid these offers and avoid all touts. Aside from putting you in a potentially risky situation, they usually end up being far more expensive than you are led to expect.

If a prearranged ride is not possible, you can get a prepaid taxi. There are usually a few options, ranging from basic to luxurious. The cheapest ones are usually OK in the daytime, but at night the risk of breakdowns is a more serious matter as some of these taxis are pretty decrepit. You are also more likely to have problems with the drivers themselves. At night, it's better to go with one of the taxi companies like EasyCab or Meru Cabs, which have various safety features like GPS and panic buttons in all the taxis.

When taking a pre-paid taxi from the airport, be sure that the registration number on your slip of paper matches the vehicle. After paying the fare at the counter, you'll typically be given two receipts with the taxi number on it, which you should check. The green receipt is for the driver, but don't give it to him until you safely reach your destination.

Taxi drivers will sometimes say that your hotel is closed for repairs even if you have a confirmed reservation, or else that the road is blocked and you can't get to it, or that the hotel is no good and they know somewhere better. Don't believe it, especially if they tell you that every hotel is booked and you will have to go to another city. For pre-paid taxis, a threat to withhold the receipt will usually be effective since they won't get paid without it. Otherwise, threaten to use the 'panic button', if there is one, or to inform the Traffic Police if they won't cooperate—or get out and take another cab. Insist on calling the hotel from the driver's phone if you don't have one, and dial the number yourself so you know you are really talking to the hotel and aren't being scammed. Never allow yourself to be taken anywhere you don't want to go.

Safe Places to Stay

Many of the best places to stay come through recommendations from other travelers. But even if a place comes highly recommended, should you feel something is wrong when you get there, look for another place.

Whenever possible, do an online check of reviews for any accommodation you are considering. If there is any hint of inappropriate behavior, look elsewhere.

If you use a service like Couchsurfing or Airbnb, avoid staying with single men unless they have a good number of positive reviews from other women and not a hint of negativity. They aren't the majority, but there are some guys who seem to think that if a girl is willing to stay at their place, they are up for sharing their bed, but that's absolutely not how those services are meant to be used! If a host acts inappropriately, get out of there and report him immediately.

Avoid accepting hospitality from strangers. For the sake of courtesy, you can thank them and say that you'd love to visit sometime, but don't make a commitment. Even if you have just spent many hours with them on the train and it feels like they are now good friends, you can't really know. If you want to meet up with them later, ask to meet at a restaurant or somewhere in public. If they keep pressing you and won't accept your excuses, don't be afraid to say a firm 'no'. Never let yourself be bullied into going with anyone. You aren't obliged to give in to their agenda.

Indians are wonderfully hospitable people, but some are so eager for visitors that they could be described as aggressively hospitable. You may meet complete strangers in airports or on trains who insist that you must come and stay with them, even within the first few minutes of your conversation! In such a culture, their motives might actually be pure, but you can't count on it.

On the other hand, if you are introduced to someone by a friend you trust and your new acquaintance invites you to stay at their house, you may want to accept, depending on the circumstances and how you feel about them. For most Indians, looking after a friend of a friend is a serious responsibility.

If you are traveling alone, avoid arriving in a new place without having a room pre-booked for the first night, especially if you will be arriving after dark. You can't rely on on a taxi or rickshaw driver to get you a decent hotel. They are likely to be far more interested in the commission they will receive for taking you there than your welfare.

When you are staying in a hotel, check the windows to make sure they can be closed and locked securely or else that there's a security grill. If the doors and windows are not secure, get a different room. Keep your door locked even when you are in the room. A rubber doorstop is a good extra security measure, especially in budget places, which don't always have good deadbolts.

Don't leave your window open at night unless it has a security screen or is safely away from any potential access.

Whenever you have to answer the door, be sure you are modestly covered. Answering the door in a flimsy nightie or bikini or underwear is extremely foolish no matter where you are. If there is a chain or peep-hole, use it before opening the door. If there is an unexpected knock on the door, call the front desk to verify who it is before you open it.

When signing a hotel register, use only your initials without a title that gives away your gender.

Avoid leaving your key lying around where someone could easily see your room number, which you don't want advertised.

Ask to have your room cleaned only when you are there. It's best not to leave a "Please Clean My Room" sign on the door when you are out.

Always get a business card or piece of paper with the address, phone number and name of your hotel or host, and keep it with you whenever you go out. You may want to get it written out in the local language, too. Be sure to mark your location on your map or app. You really don't want to venture out and realize that you don't know how to get back.

Avoid staying alone on houseboats, especially in isolated situations. Always get recommendations for safe houseboats and verify exactly what the deal includes in advance.

It's not safe to camp by yourself. Even in an extremely remote area, you can never be certain that someone has not observed where you have gone to camp. In some areas, it's not safe to camp even in a group.

No matter where you are staying, you don't want to leave your valuables in an unlocked bag. Just keep it locked all the time. If your host says, "Oh, that's not necessary here," tell them you appreciate that, but because you won't always be somewhere so safe, you simply can't afford to get out of the habit. If they don't respect that, you might wonder whether it really is so safe there. While your belongings are obviously much less important than your personal security, losing your passport and money could put you at risk in many ways. By making a habit of taking a little extra care you can avoid getting yourself in a sticky situation.

Safety on The Move

Of the various categories of taxis, radio taxis from reliable companies or the vetted taxis that you get from a five-star hotel are generally better than the ones you flag down on the road or find at general taxi stands. Even better are the taxi companies that have only women drivers. The radio cabs usually have safety features such as on-board GPS systems and panic buttons, which others may not. You can book them online or sometimes over the phone. When they confirm, they will send you a text message with the driver's name and cell number. The driver calls you when he reaches the pickup place so you don't have to wait around outside. Uber and Ola are also available in most of the large cities, and usually they are OK, though there have been some unfortunate incidents. They have added new safety features, so the situation is much better than it was.

Whenever you take a taxi or get a ride with someone you don't know, whether in a private car or on a motorbike, get the license number and driver's name, then call or text it to someone, especially if you are alone. Say where you are going and when you expect to arrive. If you can't reach anyone, then at least pretend you have, loudly repeating the information so the driver can hear. You could also take a photo and send it—and let the driver see you doing it. Or make sure someone where you are getting in knows who you are going with. Tell them you will call when you arrive. Many radio taxis now have a feature on their apps that lets you send the information to anyone you choose.

If you have hired a car for the day, always get the driver's name, cell phone number and car number. If he has to move the car while you are gone, or there is a problem, you will be able to find him. You can call the driver to pick you up right at the door if he is parked some distance away. At night, you should always do this.

Give the driver the name and address of your destination on a piece of paper—one you don't need to get back. Merely speaking the address all too often results in misunderstandings that may not get you where you intended to go. Do your best to know where you are going. Carry a map or use a maps app on your phone.

The driver may want to bring a friend or relative along, or pick up someone along the way, but don't let him get away with it, especially if you are alone or it's after dark. It's not uncommon for taxi drivers to give false excuses for taking on other passengers at your expense; and you just never know who they are. Policemen often flag down taxis for a free ride, and there's nothing you can do about it but get out and take another taxi if you feel uncomfortable.

If your driver suddenly stops on a dark, deserted road for no apparent reason, tell him in no uncertain terms to keep moving. If he seems to have bad intentions and you feel threatened, press the panic button, if there is one; or get out the pepper spray and your mobile, if you have them. In case there is a mechanical problem or flat tire, stay in the car with the doors locked while he deals with it.

Whenever you are riding in a car, keep the doors locked, especially at night. Roll the windows up if you stop at a light where there are beggars or itinerant vendors (unless you actually want to buy something), or guys on motorbikes taking too much interest in you.

If you can afford it, consider hiring a car and driver for the duration of your trip. A good driver can make for a safe and pleasant journey. However, if the driver is someone you aren't comfortable with, don't hesitate to ask for another driver—but do it as soon as possible. Avoid paying the whole amount in advance in order to keep him motivated.

You can often flag down taxis, auto-rickshaws and jeeps on the road even if they have other passengers. However, it is not advisable to do this unless there are other women or families in the car. You can also find shared jeeps and taxis in the hills and rural areas at certain taxi stands. If you want more space, ask for the whole front seat. It's almost always worth the extra rupees, especially if you are going a long distance. You can tell by the license plates and, sometimes, the color of the vehicle whether it is for hire. Taxis and vehicles for hire have yellow plates.

Many travel agents will arrange shared taxis to distant destinations. This is most common in the mountains. Look for an agent who is known to you or your friends, if possible, or who is well-recommended.

Hitchhiking is not recommended. But if for some reason you need to get a ride with strangers, be discriminating about who you accept a ride with. Don't just hop in blithely without looking carefully at the driver and any other occupants, as well as the vehicle's state of decrepitude. If you have a bad feeling, don't get in, especially if they insist. Don't get in a car with a bunch of men, even if it is the only ride around. Even two is too many if you are a woman alone.

Don't take rides from strangers at night. If you are stuck somewhere, it's almost always better to find a safe place to stay until morning rather than trying to move on. Let someone know where you are and what the situation is, even if they are far away.

Never sit in front with the driver in an auto-rickshaw; there's no way to avoid being too close.

Go for the ladies' queue for train and bus tickets, if there is one. Sometimes women can just go to the head of the queue if there isn't a special one. If you get sandwiched between men in a mixed queue, don't hesitate to tell them to give you more space. Hold your bag in front of you, and give a gentle hint with your elbows if you have to. Indians tend to crush together whenever they get in a queue, even if there is plenty of room.

When traveling alone by train, First AC is an excellent option if you can afford it. It's the most secure, and you are unlikely to have problems. The compartments are lockable, and there are attendants in the car that you can call in case of need. Also, no one can board that coach without a ticket, which is not the case with other classes. I've never experienced or seen even the slightest harassment in First AC, though I do try to avoid being in a compartment with only men. Second AC is also generally quite safe.

There is considerable debate on whether it's safe for a single woman to travel overnight in Sleeper Class. I don't recommend it. True, you are surrounded by lots of people, but many people won't intervene or get involved if something happens, especially if they perceive any risk to themselves. I'd advise finding someone to travel with or going for a higher class. At least, try to make sure you are in with families or couples.

You can ask the TTE (conductor) to move you if you feel uncomfortable; or you can ask around for someone to trade berths. Get an upper berth, if possible, to make it harder for potential molesters to get at you or for voyeurs to snap photos of you sleeping.

While violent assault of foreign women on trains is rare, harassment of some sort is not, especially in the lower classes of travel. If you are with a man, avoid kissing or other intimacies.

If you travel alone in Unreserved Class, you may want to go for the Ladies' Compartment. Most metro trains also have a women's compartment where you can escape the crush to some extent.

For overnight journeys, wear something modest and comfortable, such as a *salwar-kameez* or a *kurta-pajama* set—Indian street clothes that are as comfortable as nightwear. Cover up well when you are sleeping.

Trains heading for holy places typically have more families on board than trains between business centers, which often have a predominance of men.

Avoid taking public transportation at night—particularly night buses and overnight buses—especially if you are traveling alone. If you take an overnight bus, go for the super deluxe option, if possible. It's worth the few extra rupees. Sleeper buses generally have two berths on one side and one on the other. If you are alone, go for the single side. Semi-sleeper buses are two by two, so you don't have that option, though they normally try to avoid putting a single woman next to a man. You select your berth/ seat at the time of making a reservation, which is why it's best to make it in advance.

Absolutely avoid any bus at night that only has men on it or that is empty of passengers. Don't get on even if you have already paid for the ticket. Just don't.

Some buses have a women's section, usually at the front. If you are alone, try to sit next to other women. On crowded buses, window seats are better than the aisle, as you won't have people hanging over you. Since local buses often have people packed in like sardines, a window seat is the only place where you have any breathing room. If a local bus is too crowded, wait for a less crowded one or else opt for a private taxi or *auto-rickshaw*—or even walk, if it's not too far.

In waiting rooms, try to sit near women and families rather than by yourself. Some stations have ladies' waiting rooms, so go for those if they are available.

Avoid packing more than you can manage on your own. It's best to be mobile and not too dependent on others. If you have to struggle with your bags, you make yourself an easy target in more ways than one.

Wearing dark glasses when you are out walking around allows you to look at everyone around you without them seeing. It also helps to deflect some harassment. A wide-brim hat is also useful for hiding from unwanted stares.

It's good to wear comfortable shoes when you are out and about, so you can move quickly if need be.

Settling in for a Longer Stay

Before you choose a place to stay, check the neighborhood out thoroughly. Ask people how safe it is and if there is anything in particular to watch out for.

Once you move in, spend some time getting familiar with the neighborhood. Walk around learning where everything is, including the local police station and hospital.

Go out of your way to make friends with local women and families in your neighborhood, and don't hesitate to ask them for advice. It's safer not to be a total stranger. If they are shy, just keep smiling and saying 'hello'; eventually, they should warm up to you.

Learn a few words of the local language wherever you are. Include a few emergency expressions such as "help me." Aside from the fact that you won't be totally helpless if you have to communicate with people who don't speak English, you'll find that people you meet tend to be friendlier if you make even a tiny effort to learn their language.

When you are staying in a place for some time, don't get into a set routine, such as jogging the same route at the same time every day. Vary the time and route each day.

If you hire local people, get them verified by the police before they start working for you. It's best to hire people with solid references. Find out where they live. Get copies of their identity papers, and take photos. Don't be casual about it and don't put it off.

Be cautious with people who work for you, especially in your home. Don't put temptation in their way. Being able to hire people to work for you means you are far wealthier than they can even dream of being, so don't flaunt your wealth or leave valuables lying around.

Sex in Indian Culture

Most Indians are extremely conservative when it comes to sex. Sexual matters are considered private and are rarely discussed openly. Men and women don't mix as freely as in Western countries; and men are expected to keep a respectful distance from women they are not married to. Traditionally, they are even expected to refrain from any physical contact with their wives in public, however slight.

For a man to touch a woman in public, regardless of the intention behind it, is offensive to many people. Physical contact with a person of the opposite sex is a cultural taboo that should be respected when you are in public. Avoid greeting members of the opposite sex in public with hugs and kisses. Even holding hands is not acceptable in most places. In some places you can even be arrested for kissing in public![9]

If you are used to casually touching people when you talk to them, get out of the habit, at least when you are speaking to someone of the opposite sex. Even shaking hands with someone of the opposite sex should mostly be avoided, except in international corporate settings and other places where it's obvious that just about everyone does it. If you aren't

---

[9] Mira Kamdar tells in *Planet India* (p. 41) of a couple who were arrested and fined "in lieu of serving a ten-day jail sentence in Rajasthan for kissing each other during their wedding ceremony. . ."

comfortable when an Indian man wants to shake your hand, you can usually just *namaskar*[10] instead.

In the West, if a man wants to protect a woman, he may put his arm around her or hold her hand to send a message to other men to leave her alone. In India, it may give the impression that she is a loose woman and fair game for any man—so if you are with a man, ask him to refrain from touching you in public. By treating you in a way that Indians see as respectful, he is signaling that you are a person deserving of respect. Refrain from even looking at each other in an overly intimate way in public. Even though some Indians are rather uninhibited with their partners in public, it is generally a bad idea to do likewise.

Indians often hold hands with people of the same sex as a matter of friendship. This is not an indicator of homosexuality. If a woman takes your hand or puts her arm around you and it makes you uncomfortable, try to refrain from squirming. Just accept her action as the gesture of friendship it is meant to be, assuming there is nothing inappropriate in the touch.

Homosexuality in India was finally decriminalized as of September, 2018. However, as homosexuals in India may still face severe discrimination and

---

10 *Namaste* or *namaskar* is spoken with a slight bow and hands pressed together, palms touching and fingers pointing upwards, at about heart level.

violence, anyone engaging in homosexual activity will be safer if they are discreet about it.

Once in a while, someone may ask you about your sex life, e.g. how many people you have slept with, etc. No matter what the reality is, look shocked and refuse to answer. Questions about your sex life are highly insulting, and few Indians are so rude. You'll generally get questions like this only from young men whose hormones are raging out of control and who are desperately looking for an outlet. A positive answer—or maybe any answer—will lead them to believe they have found one, and that's likely to be an invitation to trouble of one sort or another. End the conversation and leave.

Safe Dating

If you drink, keep it moderate. Obviously, getting drunk creates plenty of opportunities for men to take advantage of you—as does getting high on drugs.

Have fun, but don't let your guard down when you are in party mode. Never worry about others ridiculing you for being cautious. It's your life and your well-being.

Be discriminating about where you go for evening entertainment and who you go with. Avoid going alone to nightclubs, bars, etc. And try to go with someone who won't be drinking.

So-called date rape drugs are often undetectable. Victims don't remember anything that occurred while under the drug's influence, even if they don't pass out. Aside from making the victims defenseless and vulnerable to assault, there can be life-threatening side effects from these drugs.

Don't leave your drink or food unattended and don't accept drinks from strangers or casual acquaintances. Don't drink anything that tastes or smells strange. Predators have been known to drug cigarettes, too, so if you smoke, bring your own.

If you suddenly begin to feel strange, sick or drunk after only one or two drinks, tell a trusted friend. Ask them to take you to a safe place away from anyone who might have spiked your drink. If you are alone, phone someone you trust to come and get you. Lock yourself in the bathroom if there is no other safe haven.

If you suspect you have been drugged and sexually assaulted, don't shower, douche or otherwise destroy any potential evidence. Go to the nearest emergency room at once so you will have evidence of the assault. Be sure to get a copy of the medical report to take to the police.

Avoid the drug scene. Drugs and safety simply do not go together. Even cannabis can put you at risk. Places known for drug abuse and rave parties, including parts of Goa, are said to have many rapes that don't get reported. This may be partly because many victims are afraid of going to jail for drug-related crimes, as the penalties can be severe. The fact that a girl has been raped while she was high probably wouldn't be protection from being prosecuted for the drugs if she took the drugs knowingly. Incidentally, drug overdose is the most common cause of death for foreigners in India.

Don't leave a bar, club or party with any guy you don't know well and aren't completely sure you can trust. Never let any guy pressure or ridicule you into going with him against your better judgment. If someone invades your personal space, ignores your protests, or tries to make you feel bad for resisting his advances, it's time to leave. Be really clear about communicating where your sexual boundaries lie. Be assertive and don't allow yourself to be pushed beyond what is acceptable. If you meet someone you'd like to know better, arrange to meet him in a safe public place, give him your email, but don't give him your address or phone number. If he turns out to be a complete jerk, you can easily block his emails.

Whenever you go out with someone, take a photo of your date and send it to a friend along with his name and the location. Tell him you want to remember this date—which, hopefully, you will. If he tells you not to do that, you should be suspicious of his motives.

Never let a date put you down or otherwise treat you badly. Lack of respect—talking dirty when you aren't inviting it, making hurtful comments, inflicting mental, physical or emotional abuse, or any rough treatment—can easily escalate to something much worse.

It's time to go if he tries to isolate you from others; if he is controlling or tries to make you feel obligated to him; if he tries to get you drunk or stoned; or if he accuses you of 'teasing' him sexually. On the other hand, if a guy seems to be going way too far out of his way to be nice to you, that might be another indicator of bad intentions.

If you need to call for help, try to do it where he can't hear you. It's a good idea to have a prearranged code set up with someone who you can call in case of emergency—something simple you can easily remember and can work into a conversation without arousing suspicion. Let them know where you are going whenever you go out on a date and ask them to keep their phone with them and turned on.

For all that, there is certainly no need to be afraid. After all, meeting new guys is a big part of the fun of traveling. Just be aware; follow the tips given above; and then get on with enjoying yourself!

If you happen to have a relaxed view of sex and are up for a nice discreet little fling, don't count on the discreet part. Expect him to brag about scoring with a foreign woman, regardless of his promises. Incidentally, you should be aware that AIDS/HIV is not uncommon, so appropriate precautions should be taken.

Dating in India is rather different than in the West. Although the situation is certainly changing, it's still the case that most marriages are arranged, and the majority of Indians don't date as we do. If they do date, it's often with a view to marriage, even if they are doing it on the sly so their families don't know until they announce that they are set on a love match. There are plenty of exceptions, of course, but this is the tradition that the majority still follows.

While many Indian men who are involved with non-Indian women are no doubt sincere in their feelings, others view them as a source of 'safe' sex (safe in the sense that they can easily be kept away from family and friends who disapprove of sex outside marriage), or 'sex education' (getting a bit of practice in before marriage), prestige, money, or a ticket to another country.

Deflecting Harassment

Sexual harassment is known by the euphemism, 'eve-teasing.' Eve-teasing, which includes everything from verbal harassment to any physical molestation short of rape, is a crime, though it's one that the culprits are seldom booked for.

Eve-teasing is more common in big cities and tourist towns in the North, especially during festivals such as Holi. Women typically are not seen during street festivals, which tend to inspire men to get drunk and, consequently, become more inclined to sexually aggressive behavior.

There is really no one right way to respond to harassment. It all depends on the situation. You always have to use your best judgment, based on your surroundings, other people present, and escape options.

When a man's behavior is inappropriate but doesn't seem dangerous, usually the best thing is to avoid eye contact, maintain silence and move away from him. Don't give him the satisfaction of a response. Any engagement or show of emotion may encourage him, no matter what you say, because that's what he's looking for. No response is no fun for him. And retaliating could easily escalate the situation beyond your control. Staying safe is always the priority.

If you feel threatened, you can use one of the safety apps on your phone that send audio, video and photos to the police and other designated recipients. Or even just pretend you are on your cell phone speaking with the police.

Although I don't generally advocate making things up, there are definitely circumstances where I wouldn't hesitate to say something like, "My [husband, boyfriend, brother…] is coming just now. He's a [big guy, martial arts expert, cop…] and he'll beat you up when he catches you, so you better get out of here fast." If you aren't sure how well the guy understands English, speak slowly and use simple words. Come up with a good line and practice it in advance so if you have occasion to use it, you can sound like you really mean it. Smiling confidently would make it more believable and effective, if you can manage it.

Crowdsourcing Assistance

Finding yourself in crowded situations from time to time is unavoidable in India, but try to stay away from demonstrations, protests, political rallies and any big crowds where there are mostly men.

If you attend a major religious festival where the crowds are dense, get up and out of the action to a place where you can observe from a safe distance. Look around for a vantage point such as a balcony, a rooftop, or a stairway where there are other women or girls. Don't be shy about asking if you can join them there. Usually, they will be delighted if you do. Not only is it safer, but you can see better than from the midst of the crowd. Big crowds always seem to attract some men who view them as an opportunity to get in a little groping.

In a crowd, the best thing is to let everyone know what the scumbag is up to. But try to keep your anger in check. Try not to swear or call him names. (Yeah, I know. Sometimes you just have to.) And avoid letting him into your personal space by responding to personal comments or throwing any back at him. Instead, call him out loudly in a way that identifies him and what he has done. Keep your voice as strong, commanding and unemotional as possible. You might say something like, "You in the black jacket, keep your hands off me!" or "You with the beard, don't insult me like that!" Being the focus of many censorious eyes is likely to make the coward slink off as quickly as possible. Crowdsourcing your defense in this way—even if no one actually does or says anything to help—will usually put a stop to the harassment.

Although many people applaud a woman who takes extreme measures against eve-teasers, remaining calm and civil may gain you more respect from those around you, and thus make them more inclined to help than to merely stand by and enjoy the entertainment. Watching a foreign girl go wild on some guy would undoubtedly be considered highly entertaining by many people.

Don't be shy about asking for help if the situation is more serious. In case help is not immediately forthcoming, call out to someone who looks reasonably intelligent and responsible, e.g. "You in the striped shirt, please call the police!" A specific call to action to an individual will have others looking to that person to do something, so it is more likely to inspire him or her to act than if you just yell, "Help!" in a general way. You might also add, "I am a guest in your country. Please help me!" Positioning yourself as a guest is always a good move in India, as guests are traditionally honored and this is an obligation that most people take seriously.

Fighting Back

Although prevention is the most important thing, all women should really learn some self-defense tactics to gain confidence in knowing how to deal with men who misbehave. Considering the amount of violence against women in the world today, every woman should know at least a little basic self-defense no matter where she is.

Predators like to target women who seem helpless and unaware of what's going on around them, so do your best to always be aware of your surroundings and to cultivate the appearance of being strong and confident even when you don't feel that way inside.

Using physical means to defend yourself should be the last resort; but if you get into a situation where you do have to defend yourself physically, do it fast, forcefully and decisively. Don't hesitate. Put up a huge struggle and make as much noise as you can. Knee him hard in the groin; deploy the pepper spray; jab him in the eye; stomp on his instep; or do whatever you can to escape.

Some women hesitate to resist because they are afraid of getting hurt, but statistics show that fighting back increases the odds of a positive outcome by around 70%.

Be careful where you take refuge following an incident, especially a serious one. Avoid ending up alone with men who might be inspired to take advantage of the situation. Remember that many men have the mindset that if you were assaulted, you must have done something to invite it—and some might be inclined to think that the invitation has just been extended to them.

Reporting a Crime

In the unlikely event that you have to report a serious crime such as physical assault or a stolen passport, notify your embassy right away.

To report a crime, you have to file an FIR (First Information Report) at the nearest police station, but avoid going there alone unless it's an all-women station. All the big cities and many smaller ones now have all-women police stations, so that's where you should go if at all possible, especially if it is a sex-related crime. Otherwise, insist on dealing with a policewoman, or at least having a woman present while you are making your report. The reason is that Indian policemen are sometimes reluctant to file an FIR for rape or eve-teasing. Many still have the attitude that the woman must have been 'asking for it.'

Note that merely recording the details in a journal is not the same as filing an FIR. When an FIR is filed, the police must start an investigation. Insist on getting a copy of the FIR. If you leave without one, it's certain that nothing will happen.

If You Are Considering Marriage

If you have fallen in love with an Indian man and are serious about him, there are some things you really must consider as objectively as possible. If he really loves you, he will almost certainly want to marry you.

You can feel confident that he is serious if he introduces you to his family. On the other hand, if he hides you from his family and friends, and keeps on making excuses, you can assume that he is just using you. And once he has had his fun with you, most likely he will marry an Indian girl as per his family's wishes. For the vast majority of Indians, marriage is an essential obligation, both for family and society.

If you are thinking seriously of marriage, do take your time to understand the cultural differences, and also to get to know his family well so you can carefully observe his family dynamics to get some idea of what you are signing up for. Spend as much time as possible with his family and see how the women of the family are treated. If you notice signs of abuse—whether physical, mental or emotional—it's highly likely that you would be abused, too. Those who have grown up in abusive families all too often think it's normal.

It's essential to ask what he expects of a wife and what he would consider to be his duties as a husband. Observe how the married women in his culture behave and are treated. Ask him about everything you notice. And be sure your thinking is the same when it comes to having and raising children. Sometimes the differences are just too much, no matter how deeply you are in love.

A request for money is a clear sign that he's not in love with you. Don't give him money for any reason. If he asks for money or keeps dropping hints, it's time to dump him, no matter what 'need' he cites. Most likely, it's a lie anyway. Give him money once and he won't stop asking for more, just like any professional beggar. He'll keep using you and exploiting you. Even such non-violent abuse can put you at risk in more ways than one.

Women's Rights in India

Women's rights and safety are taking a more and more prominent place in world consciousness and in India. While many of India's subcultures are fast becoming more liberal—which, alas, usually means more westernized—others are much slower to embrace change. Some are completely determined to resist change. I find it encouraging that outrage is growing in India over crimes against women. Probably change will continue to happen gradually for a while; but at some point, there will suddenly be a huge shift. The tipping point is approaching.

Conclusion

Staying safe in India is really not so hard. In spite of the possible problems one could encounter, relatively few Indian men are perverts or predators, or interested in harming you in any way. You don't need to be fearful. Be aware of your surroundings. Be sensible and careful, but don't worry.

There is, of course, no absolute truth when it comes to female safety. Some places are safer and more welcoming than others. A little advance research can tell you which places to avoid due to high crime rates and drug abuse or bad attitudes towards women.

Respect is essential, but respecting the culture is about much more than just safety. Many doors will open to you that might otherwise remain firmly closed and hidden. And you will find people much more friendly, open and ready to help you. It's one of the keys to experiencing the best of India.

May your time in India be safe and happy!

About the Author

JD Viharini is an American woman who has made India her home. Preferring to remain anonymous, she writes under the pseudonym, JD Viharini, which is derived from an epithet of Ganga, *Jambu-dvipa-viharini*, meaning 'one who wanders around enjoying India'. That's her, for sure!

Inspired in her twenties by the rich Vedic literature and traditions of India (*Veda* means 'Knowledge of Life,' and the Vedas are the basis of most Indian religions and cultures), she eventually acquired a Master's degree in Vedic Studies. With this deep understanding of the roots of the Indian way of life, she began traveling to India more than three decades ago.

She has lived in India for more than a decade and has spent many more traveling extensively throughout the country—mostly solo—first class, sardine class, and everything in between. She's been sick and learned how to stay well; resided in big cities and remote villages; stayed in primitive guest houses and opulent hotels; lived with traditional families and studied at ashrams. She has learned how to travel and live, happily and comfortably, in this most magnificent of countries. Now she wants to share what she has learned in order to help others enjoy India to the max.

Printed in Great Britain
by Amazon

32495347R00052